DATE			

A HOLIDAY BOOK

Valentine's Day

BY ELIZABETH GUILFOILE

ILLUSTRATED BY GORDON LAITE

GARRARD PUBLISHING COMPANY
CHAMPAIGN, ILLINOIS

Holiday Books are edited under
the educational supervision of

Charles E. Johnson, Ed.D.
Associate Professor of Education
University of Illinois

Published in Champaign, Illinois, by Garrard Publishing Company
Manufactured in the United States of America

Library of Congress Catalog Card Number: 65-10086

505

Contents

1
Saint Valentine

Every year, on February 14, the mailman's bag is stuffed with valentine cards decorated with lace, hearts, cupids and flowers. Doorbells ring, and there stand messengers with boxes of candy and bouquets of flowers. At school, boys and girls drop valentines into boxes for each other.

There is reason for all this fun and excitement. The messages mean that your friends are thinking about you. On this day they tell of their love and friendship in many ways. The gifts and cards all mean the same thing. They are valentines.

Many people do not know why February 14 is called Valentine's Day. Most people believe it got its name from a man named Valentine who lived 1700 years ago. He was a priest in Rome when Christianity was a new religion. He was put to death for teaching Christianity. Afterwards he was called a saint.

There are many legends about Saint Valentine. Legends are stories that are handed down from the past. The legends about Saint Valentine may not be true, but they show how people felt about him.

One legend tells why Saint Valentine is

the patron saint of lovers. The Roman soldiers did not want to leave their homes to fight the emperor's wars. Claudius II, who was the emperor then, ordered the young men not to marry. He thought that if they did not have homes, they would be willing to go away and fight.

Valentine felt sorry for the unhappy young men and their sweethearts. He married many of them secretly. So even today, sweethearts celebrate in his honor.

Another legend tells why messages are sent on this day. The story says that Valentine raised beautiful flowers in his garden. He gave many of them to the children who lived nearby. Later, the emperor had Valentine put in prison because he wouldn't preach about the Romans' gods.

The children missed Valentine. They
picked flowers, made little bouquets and
tied notes to them. The notes said that
they loved him. They tossed the bouquets
through Valentine's prison window.

Valentine was put to death, and later,
people remembered this story. They began
to write to their friends on the anniversary

of his death—February 14—saying that they loved them. Sometimes they sent flowers too. They called these "valentines."

While Valentine was in prison, the jailer's daughter became his friend. She was blind. The priest prayed for her, and she got back her sight. Before he died, Valentine wrote a good-by letter to the little girl. He signed it, "From your Valentine."

We like to believe these legends. They make Saint Valentine real to us.

2
A Roman Festival
of Early Spring

Some Valentine's Day customs go back
to an old, old Roman holiday, the
Lupercalia. This festival was celebrated
long before Valentine lived. It began
when Rome was a tiny village. Fierce
wolves lived in the woods nearby. The
Romans called upon one of their gods,
Lupercus, to keep the wolves away. They

11

held a festival in Lupercus' honor every year on February 15. They played games, sang and danced for him.

Years passed. Rome grew into a town, then into a city. The wolves had been driven away long ago, but the people kept the festival. It was still celebrated in Valentine's time.

One of the customs the young people liked was name-drawing. The names of the Roman girls were written on slips of paper and put into a jar. Each young man drew a slip. The girl whose name he drew was to be his sweetheart for a year.

No one knows how or when this name-drawing started. Drawing names could not keep wolves away. Probably boys and girls started the custom for fun. The middle of February was early spring in Rome, and everyone was thinking of sweethearts.

After Saint Valentine died, more and more Romans became Christians. The Christian priests moved the spring holiday from February 15 to February 14, Valentine's Day. Now the holiday honored Saint Valentine instead of Lupercus.

The priests tried to make the name-drawing fit in with Christian ways. Saints' names were written on the slips of paper. Each boy and girl drew a name and tried to copy that saint's life.

However, people liked the old custom best. Soon they went back to it. Again the boys drew girls' names. Now the little name slips were called valentines. When a boy drew a girl's name he said she was his valentine.

So Saint Valentine's Day became a romantic spring festival.

3
Old Valentine's Day Customs

Rome became powerful and conquered much of Europe, including Britain. Slowly the British people took over the Roman holidays. After the Romans left, the British continued to celebrate Valentine's Day.

In England it was much colder in February than it was in Rome. However, everyone knew that spring was on the way.

The first birds had come back from the south. Soon they would be busy making their nests. Some people thought that the birds chose their mates on Saint Valentine's Day.

Young people hoped to find their own mates on Valentine's Day. They chanted magic charms and spells, trying to make their wishes come true. This pagan magic had been added to the holiday by the British.

Sometimes a girl went all alone to a cemetery at midnight. She carried a handful of hempseed. As the clock struck twelve, she scattered the seed on the ground and sang:

"Hempseed I sow, hempseed I mow,
  He that will my true love be
  Rake this hempseed after me."

Then she ran home. While she ran she looked back over her shoulder. She hoped to see her true love following her. That meant they were sure to be married within a year.

Other kinds of magic were tried on Valentine's Eve. One young lady pinned four bay leaves to the corners of her pillow, and one in the middle. Then she dreamed of her sweetheart. She thought that meant she would be married to him soon. She also tried something else.

"I boiled an egg hard and took out the yolk and filled it with salt, and when I went to bed ate it, shell and all, without speaking or drinking."

The next morning she kept her eyes shut tight, until her sweetheart came to the house. *"For I would not have seen another man before him for all the world,"* she said. Each girl thought the first boy she saw on Valentine's Day would become her husband.

Saint Valentine's Day came to be celebrated in most of the countries of Europe. Sicily is an island south of Italy. There a young girl would stand at her window for half an hour before sunrise. If no one went by, she believed she would not be married that year. If she saw a man pass, she thought she would marry him or someone who looked like him.

In Germany the girls tried another way of learning whom they would marry. They planted onions on Saint Valentine's Day. Each girl tagged several dry onions with the names of young men. She put the onions in a corner near the fireplace. She thought she would marry the man whose onion sprouted first.

A French princess, Madame Royale, named her palace "The Valentine." She had grand valentine parties in the early 1600's. There were dancing and name-drawing. The princess did not draw a name. She chose her own partner, but she made her guests draw names. Each knight gave flowers to the lady whose name he drew. He gave her flowers at each dance they attended that year.

Valentine parties became popular in many wealthy French homes. The young ladies and gentlemen put verses into a valentine box. They put their names into the box, too, on different slips. Then each person drew a name and a verse. The gentleman read his verse to the lady. She read hers to him. Often the verse did not match the person and everyone laughed.

Rich Frenchmen gave expensive presents

to the ladies whose names they drew. Rich Englishmen gave expensive presents too. In 1677, the Duke of York bought a ring for his valentine. It cost 800 English pounds, equal to thousands of American dollars.

Samuel Pepys, who lived in England in the 1600's, wrote in his diary every day. Once he wrote that he had drawn the name of a little girl for Saint Valentine's Day. *"I am glad. If she were a grown-up young lady I would have to give her a more expensive present."*

In the 1700's, the custom of sending expensive gifts was stopped. An English minister wrote in his diary, *"This being Valentine's Day gave 52 children of this parish as usual 1 penny each."*

The English children had fun in their own way on Valentine's Day. They ran about singing such greetings as this:

"Curl your locks as I do mine;
Two before and three behind.
So Good Morning, Valentine,
Hurra! Hurra! Hurra!"

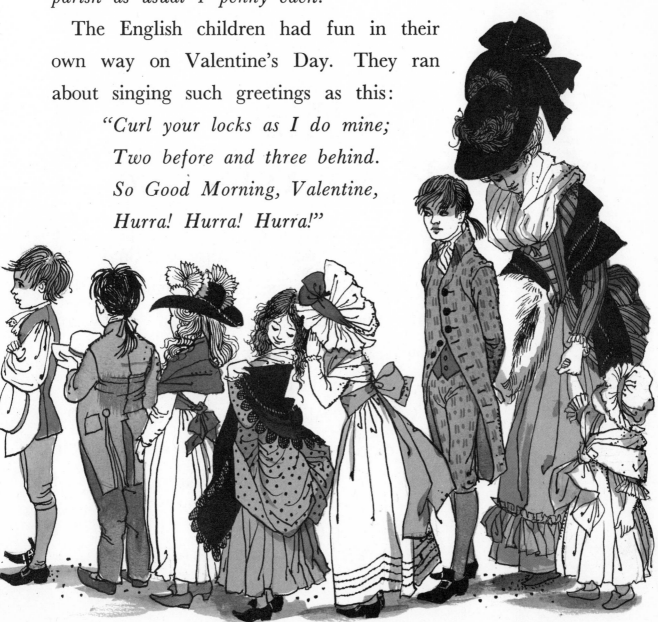

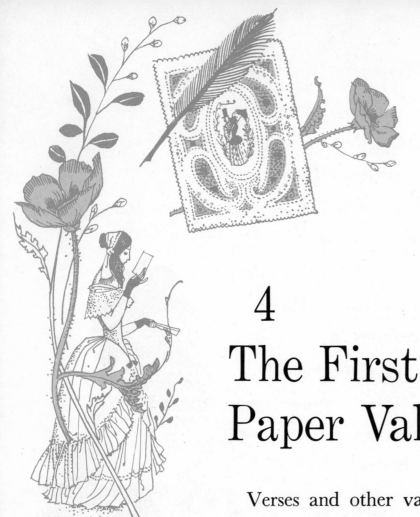

4
The First
Paper Valentine

Verses and other valentine greetings were popular even in the Middle Ages. At that time few people could read or write. Lovers usually said or sang their valentines to their sweethearts.

Written valentines began about 1400. The oldest one we know of was made in 1415. A Frenchman, Charles, Duke of

Orleans, was captured by the English in a battle. He was put in prison in the Tower of London. There he wrote valentine poems. Many of them were saved and can be seen today in the British Museum.

The idea of paper valentines spread throughout Europe. They began to take the place of valentine gifts. Paper valentines were especially popular in England.

For a long time valentines were made by hand. The sender often wrote his own message in verse. Sometimes he used pretty colored paper and even colored ink.

In the early 1800's, factories began to make valentines. Black and white pictures were printed on pretty paper. Some of them were painted by workers in the factory. But most people bought plain pictures and did their own painting. Some valentines had verses printed on them.

Others left room for the sender to write his own message.

Then valentines became more fancy. At first, the fancy valentines were trimmed with ribbons and real lace. About 1840, factories began to make paper lace. A long strip of paper was run through great rollers. The rollers stamped or cut a lacy pattern on the edges of the paper. Then the strip was cut into pieces the size of valentines.

These valentines were only one page. Workers painted pictures in the middle of the paper. Other workers sewed or glued ornaments onto the pictures or the paper lace edges.

Later, factories made folded valentines. The inside page had a printed verse, and the front page was a picture. The edges were of paper lace. Sometimes workers

pasted two or three layers of lace on the front, one above the other. Little strips of paper held each layer above the next. The center was open. This made a frame for the picture.

Sometimes there were ornaments on each layer of lace. These ornaments were made of silk, satin, velvet or spun glass. Even feathers were used!

One factory bought tiny cloth roses for ornaments. Each rose was no larger than a pea. They were so well made that the petals looked like real rose petals. These flowers were made by ladies who never got valentines themselves. They were nuns in a French convent.

Making valentines by hand was slow and costly. The manufacturers began to make cheaper valentines. They stamped the pictures and ornaments directly on the cards.

By the end of the nineteenth century, valentines could be bought for a few pennies. They were made entirely by machines. The colors were bright. The paper lace was coarse. These were quite different from the lovely, dainty valentines that were made earlier.

5
Valentine Symbols and the Story of Cupid

The ornaments that decorate valentines are symbols of love and friendship.

Ornaments for early valentines were made by hand. Each had a special meaning. A fan meant "Open up your heart." A ribbon meant "You are tied up," or "You are my girl." Lace is the same word, in Latin, as "net." So a lace ruffle on a valentine meant, "You have caught my heart in a net."

At valentine parties romantic symbols were sometimes hidden in a cake. Each guest got a slice and, if he was lucky, a symbol. The symbol told his fortune. Sometimes the symbols were put in gift packages instead.

Rice meant a wedding. A ring meant a wedding too, or an engagement. A coin meant the person would marry someone wealthy. Sometimes a boy got a red mitten. "To get the mitten" meant his girl did not like him.

Hearts are the most common romantic symbol. Candy, cookies, and even cakes are made in heart shapes for valentine parties.

Little hearts appear on valentines themselves. So do pictures of flowers, butterflies,

birds and baby lambs. These are symbols of spring. Two hands clasped together mean love. Wedding rings and lovers' knots tie the couple together.

Angels and children bless a happy marriage. Harps and lyres play romantic music.

One of the most famous valentine symbols is Cupid with his bow and arrow.

He goes back to Roman times. Here is a story the Romans told about him.

Cupid was the son of a beautiful goddess, Venus. Wherever Venus went Cupid went too. He was a gay little god and he liked to see people happy. He went around shooting gold-tipped arrows into the hearts of humans. Then they fell in love.

Venus, his mother, had a golden mirror. She looked into it every day. She saw the most beautiful face in the world. One day Cupid found his mother crying. "Alas," she said, "I have lost my golden mirror!"

Cupid went in search of the mirror. He looked here and he looked there, but he could not find it. Then he flew over a meadow where some sheep were grazing. Among the sheep stood a shepherd.

As Cupid looked down, beams of light flashed up into his eyes. He saw that the

light came from something in the shepherd's hand. The little god flew low over the shepherd and his flock. The sheep were startled by the sound of his wings. They began to bleat and run away.

The shepherd looked up. Cupid saw his rough, bearded face. He saw, too, what the shepherd held in his hand. It was Venus' golden mirror. The little god was

angry. He cried out, "You have dared to look at your ugly face in my beautiful mother's mirror!"

He struck the mirror from the shepherd's hand. It fell to the ground and broke into hundreds of pieces. Plants with beautiful blossoms sprang up where the mirror had broken. Later the people called the flowers "Venus' Looking-Glass."

6
Novelties and Comics

During the 1800's, valentine styles kept changing. Some valentines were strange, some comic, some beautiful. The beautiful ones were designed by artists.

One English artist was Kate Greenaway. She became famous for her illustrated verses for children.

Kate earned her first money drawing and painting valentines and Christmas cards. She sold her first valentine design for $15. The company that manufactured the valentine sold 25,000 copies of it.

Kate Greenaway liked the clothes that people had worn in earlier times. She drew little girls in long dresses and capes, and straw hats with ribbons. She also designed

clothes for boys. Sometimes she made boy dolls or girl dolls and designed costumes for them. Then she painted pictures from these models.

People liked Kate's pictures. Little girls began to wear dresses like those in her picture books and valentines.

In the mid-1800's, Englishmen were digging for gold in Australia. They ordered expensive valentines from England for their wives and sweethearts. The miners liked a lot of real gold in the decorations. One valentine, made for the miners, was two feet long. It had rows of colored pictures and borders of gold and silver lace.

Valentines with moving parts began to be popular. Usually there was a stick of cardboard in the back. This stick made some part of the valentine move. Often doors or windows opened. One valentine

showed two lovers walking through a
churchyard. When the church door was
opened, a wedding could be seen inside.
Another mechanical valentine had a man
pushing a baby carriage.

One novelty valentine had a stuffed
hummingbird pasted onto it. Another had
a little package of perfume. Still another
had a lady's night cap. This valentine said,
*"Good night Dear! And in your thoughts
forget me not."*

Sometimes paper dolls were pasted on the valentine blanks. The dolls were dressed in real clothes.

Along with these novelties, the comic valentines were popular. They poked fun at people or at their jobs. The pictures were like those in cartoons. The colors were bright and often ugly. These comics could be mean but they were amusing too, and many of them were sold.

Here is one that was sent to a proud girl who liked pretty clothes:

"*Not a thought was ever bred*
In her vain and empty head,
Dresses, hats and furbelows,
These are all the things she knows."

7
Valentines in America

Valentines probably came to this country with the earliest English settlers. Puritans from England settled Massachusetts Bay Colony in 1630. John Winthrop was their first governor. Before he left for America he started a letter to his wife: *"February 14, 1629. Thou must be my valentine."*

The oldest valentines known in this country were sent to the colonists from their friends in Europe. One valentine found in an old collection was sent by Edward Sangon of London in 1684. The message began, *"Good morrow Vallentine."*

At first the colonists were so busy battling the wilderness that they did not have time to make many valentines. But as the years went by valentines became more common. During the winter months in America there was little farm work. A young man could spend many hours making a valentine if he wished. When February 14 came he folded his valentine and sealed it with sealing wax. Then he delivered it himself. Mail in colonial times was expensive and irregular.

Men often sent valentines as proposals of marriage. Sometimes the young lady sent

one in return, saying yes. Of course, there were far more valentines of all kinds sent by men than by women.

Some of the senders were fine artists. Their valentines were beautifully drawn and colored. The writing was beautiful too.

Cutouts were popular. The paper was folded several times and then cut with scissors or a sharp knife. When it was unfolded, it showed a design.

The people from Germany who settled Pennsylvania made valentines with fancy cutout work. They painted them in bright colors. Sometimes they pricked out lacy designs with pins.

Often a lock of hair was enclosed in a valentine. It was meant as a love token. Silhouettes were also popular. The young man sent a silhouette picture of himself. If the young lady liked it she might hang the picture on the wall.

Books called valentine writers were sold
as early as 1823. These had many valentine
verses. People who could not think up
their own greetings copied verses from the
book.

These lines, used in the 1700's, are still
popular today.

"*The rose is red, the violet blue,*
Lilies are fair and so are you."

Sometimes the sender folded his valentine
this way and that, as he wrote his verse.

Some words would be on one fold, some on another. Then he opened the paper. The lady who got the valentine had to figure out how to fold it back again so she could read the message.

In the late 1700's, stores started selling special letter paper for valentines. There were decorations printed around the edges. The sender wrote his verses in the middle.

One of the first stores to sell imported valentines was in Worcester, Massachusetts. It belonged to a Mr. Howland who sold writing supplies and books. Someone sent Mr. Howland's daughter, Esther, a lacy valentine from England in 1847. It was the first English valentine she had ever seen. Her friends thought it was beautiful.

Her father decided to import some valentines to sell. Esther was so pleased with them she made one of her own.

Mr. Howland did not import any more valentines. Instead, he imported paper lace, colored paper and paper flowers. Esther wanted to make the valentines herself.

Soon Esther had hundreds of orders. How could she make that many valentines before Saint Valentine's Day?

Her friends helped her. One girl cut out the pictures. Another glued the tiny

paper flowers to the paper lace. Another painted in leaves and vines and flowers. Soon all the orders were filled.

The valentine business grew. Esther hired many helpers who worked in her home. They sat at long tables under a skylight on the top floor. Each girl did one part of the work and then passed the valentine to the next.

Later, Esther bought machinery to do some of the work. She also manufactured Christmas cards, May baskets and other holiday favors. Soon her business was earning $100,000 a year.

Some of Esther Howland's things were expensive. A young man had paid ten dollars for one of her May baskets. He sent it to a girl and asked her to marry him. The girl said no. She would not marry anyone who spent money so foolishly!

8
Yesterday and Today

Esther Howland's fancy valentines made Valentine's Day more popular than it had been before. Soon many factories were making elaborate lacy valentines.

In 1847, the post office began to sell 5 and 10 cent stamps. One of these stamps would take a valentine any place in the United States. That year, three million valentines were sold.

Many valentines were sent to soldiers during the Civil War. A lot of these were comics. The pictures were funny but often the messages were romantic.

In the 1880's, valentines became more elaborate than ever. The centers were often stuffed satin, the edges trimmed with lace tassels. There were "shadow boxes" with valentine scenes inside.

Ladies as well as men sent valentines by this time. So did children. This valentine verse was printed in a children's magazine, *St. Nicholas,* in 1877.

A Valentine

(by A.E.C.)

If you will be my valentine,
My charming little dear,
The sun can never help but shine
Throughout the coming year.

If you will be my valentine,
You'll see in all your walks
Fresh lemon drops on every twig,
And peanuts on the stalks.

But if from you I never hear,
Nor even get a line,
I'll ask some other nicer girl
To be my valentine.

Special valentines were made for children. They liked the mechanical ones imported from Germany. In the early 1900's, automobiles were new and exciting. So were automobile valentines with wheels that really moved.

Manufacturers hired clever people to write their verses. Here is a famous one written by Carolyn Wells in 1907.

There was a young fellow named
*   Allan Tyne*
Who proposed to the lovely
*   Miss Ballantyne;*
When the lady said "Yes,"
He said, "Well I guess
Miss Ballantyne's Allan Tyne's
*   Valentine."*

Amusing verses like this are very popular today. There is a new kind of comic valentine that looks much like an ordinary

53

greeting card. It is well designed and
printed. The verse inside may sound mean
but it is so funny you can't help laughing.
It is meant as a joke.

There are still many of the old-fashioned
sentimental valentines too. They may not
be as lovely and delicate as in the past
but they still say "From your valentine."
And they still mean "I love you."

There are special valentines for parents, children, cousins, teachers and friends. And there are boxes of valentine parts for children to put together. Children today send more valentines than grownups.

Probably Americans send more valentines than all other countries put together. In 1963, we bought 550 million of them. That is nearly three times as many people as we have in this country!

9
Valentine Parties

Name drawing was a popular Valentine's Day custom in early New England. One old valentine of colonial days says:

"When I did draw my valentine,

It was my fortune you to find."

Miss Anna Green Winslow lived in Massachusetts in the late 1700's. One Valentine's Day she went to a party. She hoped to draw a fine gentleman's name.

She was cross when she drew the name of a farmer instead. She wrote in her diary: "*Valentine Day. My valentine was an old country plow-joger.*"

The English colonists had brought the custom of telling fortunes with them. They cut apples in two and counted the seeds with this verse.

"*One I love, two I love, three I love,
    I say
Four I love with all my heart.
Five I cast away.
Six he loves, seven she loves, eight
    they both love;
Nine he comes, ten he tarries,
Eleven he courts, twelve he marries.*"

The Dutch people of old New York celebrated *Vrouwen Dagh* or Women's Day in February. Young ladies ran about carrying ropes. They beat any young men they met. The blows did not hurt, but the young men made a lot of noise. It was great fun for everyone.

Later, only children followed this custom. The girls chased the boys and beat them. In one school the boys asked for *Mannen Dagh*—Men's Day. They said they wanted to get even with the girls.

As valentines became more and more popular so did valentine parties. Children in the nineteenth century played "Drop the Handkerchief" at their parties. The boy kissed the girl who dropped the handkerchief, but he had to catch her first. "Post Office," another kissing game, was also popular.

Grownups had valentine dinners and
dances. Sometimes the dancers wore masks
and dressed like famous couples: Jack and
Jill, Cinderella and the Prince, the King
and Queen of Hearts.

In 1894, a fashionable lady made place
cards of folding hearts for her party. The
menu was printed inside the hearts.

There were cream of love apples (cream of tomato soup), turtledoves (ice cream in the shape of birds) and kisses (fancy sugar cookies).

Today we still keep many of the old valentine customs. Girls tell fortunes. They count the buttons on their clothes, saying:

"Rich man, poor man, beggar man, thief,
Doctor, lawyer, merchant, chief."

The last button is supposed to tell which man the girl will marry.

Boys and girls have valentine parties at school or home. They make heart chains of red paper for decorations. Sometimes gold and silver arrows are used. These are Cupid's arrows. Paper doilies are often trimmed with hearts or flowers. Roses and forget-me-nots are symbols of love.

Strawberry, raspberry or peppermint ice cream is often used, as red is the valentine color. Cakes, cookies and candies are made in heart shapes and decorated in pink or red. The valentine symbols are still the same.

There is a valentine box at the valentine party. It is usually made out of an old hat box or a big shoe box decorated with crepe paper.

Sometimes the valentines have no names on them. Each boy or girl takes a turn reaching into the box. Or a "postmaster" passes the valentines out.

The valentine box is even older than valentines. When we draw valentines from a box, we are like the Romans who drew names from a jar. We are keeping a custom that began more than 2,000 years ago. It is wonderful to think how many, many people have said, *"Be my valentine."*